Walking through the Hallways of Faith

Walking through the Hallways of Faith

Bishop Johnny M. Williams Sr.

Co-Author:
Gracie Williams Lyman

Contributor:
Dr. Ruth Williams

2016

Copyright © 2016 by Johnny M. Williams Sr.

All rights reserved. This book or any portion thereof may not be reproduced or used in any manner whatsoever without the express written permission of the publisher except for the use of brief quotations in a book review or scholarly journal. Published in the United States by N. Jones Enterprise LLC, Woodbridge.

All scriptures are quoted from the King James Version, except where otherwise noted.

First Printing: 2016

ISBN #:

N. Jones Enterprise LLC
http://www.njonesenterprise.org

Ordering Information:

U.S. trade bookstores and wholesalers: Please contact N. Jones Enterprise LLC. Email: info@njonesenterprise.org

Dedication

To my wife Ruth and my sister Gracie Williams Lyman, who supported and assisted me in writing about the supernatural events that my Heavenly Father has performed in my life.

It is because of you I can share my story so that everyone who reads it will understand that God is a loving, caring and promise-keeping God.

Acknowledgements

During my years at the 'Rock', I was not without help. I was not without assistants and 'trainees.' Many moved forward from under my tutelage, and became great spiritual leaders, teachers and pastors. I learned from them as I instructed them:

Dr. Donald R. Whittaker now founding pastor of Agape Faith Church in Bossiere City, Louisiana.

Pastor Alex Wesco now pastors a great church in Picayune, Mississippi.

Pastor James Rivers Willis, Sr. serves as pastor of Carver Desire Baptist Church in New Orleans, Louisiana.

The late Pastor Joseph Merrill also was a pastor of the New Kingdom Baptist Church in New Orleans, Louisiana.

Minister Joseph Singletary and my sister, Evangelist Gracie Williams Lyman, are also pastors in the New Orleans area.

Bishop Donald R. Williams, Sr., my nephew, serves as pastor of Potomac Baptist Church in Washington, D.C.

My great-nephew, Bishop Lionel J. Traylor, is the pastor of The Epicenter Church in Jackson, Mississippi.

Special acknowledgements to the late Rev. Dr. Joseph Clifford (J.C.) Profit Jr., former pastor of the Stronger Hope Baptist Church of New Orleans, Louisiana, who served as a great mentor to me.

Table of Contents

Dedication..v

Acknowledgements................................vii

Preface..1

Foreword...5

Introduction..9

Chapter 1 – The Shunammite Woman's Son..13

Chapter 2 – Philip's Blindness...................21

Chapter 3 – Elisha's Willingness...............29

I Believe I will Testify................................37

Chapter 4 – The Will of My Father 41

Chapter 5 – Mary's Obedience..................47

Chapter 6 – A Time of Pentecost...............57

Chapter 7 – Signs and Wonders 61

I Believe I Will Testify...............................69

Chapter 8 – The Waters of Faith 77

Chapter 9– The Chapter of Ruth 83

Chapter 10–Revelations 95

Words to Walk by 99

Notes: 101

Preface

Now our faith is: Confidence, Trust, Belief, and Assurance in the Almighty God.

The Christian's life is a walk and lifestyle of faith. A believer cannot have a personal relationship with the Creator without first believing He is God and that He truly exists and is the omnipresent Savior.

Faith and trust in God's word are what we hold on to until God delivers what we have trusted and believed Him for. Our faith is the evidence of things not seen but shall come to pass. According to St. John 16:23, "Whatsoever I ask the Father in Jesus' name He will give it to us."

We often times hear believers say "the Lord will work it out." However, faith is believing that He has already worked it out when He said on the cross at Calvary, "It's finished." Faith is what makes the blood of Jesus work.

The reason He came to earth had been accomplished and all of our needs were taken care of at Calvary. We only need to believe and accept it.

The believer can trust in God with all his heart. God keeps every one of His promises. Whatever He has promised, He stands on His word. We have assurance of His faithfulness.

Hebrews 11:16 states, "But without faith it is impossible to please Him (God): for He that cometh to God must believe that He is, and that He is a rewarder of them that diligently seek Him." Many refer to Hebrews chapter 11 as the Faith Chapter in the Bible because in this chapter we are given many examples of heroes who trusted God and walked by faith. However, as you read this book, I encourage you to view every chapter in the Holy Bible as a faith chapter.

Walking through the Hallways of Faith

Trust God to lead you as He brings you 'Through the Hallways of Faith' to each opened door in your life.

Let us continuously pray, "Lord increase our faith."

-Gracie Williams Lyman

Bishop Johnny Marlon Williams Sr.

Foreword

Having been a part of the Williams Family now for nearly three decades, I must confess that my heart and spirit were refreshed as I read this book in its entirety – what was especially refreshing for me was the many nuggets and information that I learned for the first time or in greater detail.

The many personal testimonials and firsthand accounts of events that are shared in the pages of this work are sure to uplift, encourage and usher any believer down the "Hallways of Faith" and towards the next door or destination in the life journey of that particular believer.
I wish to personally salute Bishop Johnny M. Williams, Sr. for a job well done. By preparing and leaving this brief written record, multitudes of admirers and young ministers will have a valuable resource and will be provoked unto good works as they receive a peek into the life and ministry of the Bishop. I refer to this book as a "brief written record" because it is not possible to fit

every moment of significance in the pages of any size book – no one should expect any book to include every outstanding and memorable moment in the life of an individual who has a nearly fifty (50) year record of consistent service and ministry to the Body of Christ.

As I read this book (twice), I was especially blessed to have been an eye witness to some of the things chronicled within its pages – namely the famous "Church on Wheels". In addition, although I was only a young teenager, I vividly remember some of those wonderful worship experiences at Greater Little Rock and the tremendous respect that Bishop Williams' ministry commanded. And more recently, I certainly recall the series of events regarding the Bishop's health scare, when God allowed Dr. J. M. Williams, Sr. to "become" the miracle that he has so faithfully preached and proclaimed for these many years. Of course, no one can tell the story like the Lovely Leading Lady of Living

Faith Baptist Cathedral – Dr. Ruth Washington Williams (Hint, Hint – Chapter 9 is an absolute MUST READ!!!).

I believe that every person who has been so fortunate as to have been a part of the life and ministry of Bishop Johnny M. Williams, Sr. shares this sentiment; This book serves as a reminder of the many reasons that we are so grateful to Almighty God for having placed such a wonderful man among us and our hearts shall be eternally grateful for the many ways in which the preaching, teaching, guidance and genuine concern of the Bishop has given to each of us the strength to continue walking through the Hallways of Faith. I humbly salute the Bishop and am Godly Proud of our Kingdom Connection.

Bishop Kevin J. Boyd, Sr., D.Min
Pastor – The Apostolic Church At New Orleans (CANO)

Bishop Johnny Marlon Williams Sr.

Introduction

Walk by Faith... Not by Sight
"Now faith is the substance of things hoped for, the evidence of things not seen. For by it the elders obtained a good report." Hebrews 11:1-2

At this point in my life, my memory escapes me at times, but I believe while I am experiencing some moments of recognizance, I should be the first to write about my story.

Saints of God, when I speak of *Walking through the Hallways of Faith*, I speak as an ambassador of Christ. My feet have walked the floors of faith and hope in God. Even in recent years, as fate would have it, my health suddenly failed and I died en route to the hospital; God spoke life back into my body and I am alive to testify of His healing and resurrecting power.

It is because of no goodness of my own I am here, but only because of God's mercies. I believe I owe it to God to share my testimonies of His faithfulness.

I confess, I have not always responded in faith but God has always been faithful toward me. I have not always understood how God was going to provide for me, but

He has never failed me. Even while trusting in God, I have experienced many highs and many lows, many failures and many successes but I am blessed because the eyes of the Lord never left me.

As you read this book, I encourage you Saints of God to receive the wisdom in this book and understand that God is real and that a relationship with Him is important for any encounter in your life. When you are at your lowest point or highest point of your life, He promised never to leave nor forsake the believer because He is the solution to every dilemma.

I encourage you to always *walk with God through the hallways faith*.

Bishop Johnny Marlon Williams Sr.

Chapter 1 – The Shunammite Woman's Son

2 Kings 4:19

"And he said unto his father, My head, my head. And he said to a lad, Carry him to his mother."

In the year of 1946, many historical events were boiling in the heat of the United States: Jackie Robinson, the first African American Major League Baseball second baseman, arrived in Daytona Beach, Florida for spring training with the Montreal Royals of the Class AAA International League; Harry Truman was the 33rd President of the United States of America; and Joe Louis won the heavyweight boxing title. In the southern state of Louisiana, Jimmie Davis sat in the Governor's seat and in August 1946, in the small rural town of Watson, Louisiana, a baby boy was born.

My parents, Eddie and Lucille Jackson Williams named me Johnny. Later, my name was legally changed to Johnny Marlon Williams.

I was the tenth child and the fifth son of seventeen children. Many people in the neighborhood or as we refer to it as "on the outside looking in," said I was just another little black boy born to a poor family with already more than enough family members in the household and more than enough mouths to feed. No doubt we were poor, but my humble beginning of being born to parents of share croppers was by no means an indication of the great destiny God had already planned for my life.

From my birth, my family members said I was 'unique'. Some of my older siblings said they knew even when I was a baby that I was different and special. My sister Gracie often told me my "characteristics were pronounced and distinctive." She said, "I do not think our parents had an inkling that their son was born to be a special servant of the Most High God. He is chosen and assigned by God to be anointed for His Kingdom's purpose," Gracie concludes.

Two of my older sisters, Mary and Alberta, catered to me relentlessly and as a young child they spoiled me unduly because they said there was just something exceptional about me.

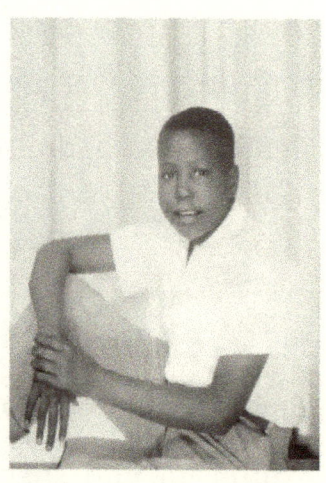

My walk of faith started with my mother being an example of faith before me and following her example. When I was five years old, my oldest sister, Loretta was preparing to mop the wooden floors in our home. During that time, floors were cleaned by mopping with lye and water. Loretta opened the container of lye and sat it down. In a matter of seconds, I picked up the can of lye and drank some of it. Alarmed at what had happened, Loretta and the family rushed me to Charity Hospital in New Orleans. The ninety miles trip from Watson, Louisiana to New Orleans was very stressful. But, my mother prayed the entire way to the hospital. She knew how to pray even before she acknowledged her calling as a prayer intercessor.

God answered my mother's prayer. Not only was my life preserved after drinking the poisonous chemical, but I had no side effects, and there was no permanent damage to my mouth, vocal cords, throat, or intestinal tract. My mother never took credit for the miracle God performed in my life. She continued to pray and praise Him and God continued to reward her faith.

It was only a few years later when Satan attacked my body a second time. For some reason, I began to have severe migraine headaches. This phase in my early life reminds me of the Shunammite woman's son, in 2 Kings 2:19, who one day ran to his father complaining, "My head hurts. My head hurts." So, his father told one of the servants to take the child to his mother. My migraine headaches were also very intense. The extreme pain would stay over my left eye until I'd regurgitate.

My sister, Mary, recalls, "We were living in the Haydel Heights community in New Orleans. Sometimes his headaches would be so severe, if it were raining, he would go outside, walk in the rain, lay on the ground, and roll in the water and mud trying to seek some relief. When he went into the house, I would clean the mud off him and change his clothes. That was a painful time for him."

Many times I did as the Shunammite woman's son. I went to my mother and I would lay my head in her lap. As she gently rubbed my head, I could hear her praying and asking the Lord to heal me from the excruciating migraine pain.

At that time, my mother did not have a remedy to stop the pain. But, she had faith that if God restored life back to the Shunammite woman's son, who died because of his severe headaches, certainly He could spare me from death and cure me from Satan's attack with the migraine headaches, and God did just that. The Almighty God commanded healing on my life, and His deliverance and power brought me through those painful migraine episodes.

My mother never stopped being a demonstrator of prayer and faith in God. She was not wealthy neither was she well educated, but her greatest asset was her God and her best education was in the wisdom she received from Him. I believe God spared my life from sudden childhood tragedies to perform something greater in my life in the future. I believe He was preparing me for a relationship with Him through the example of my mother.

When I was approximately 12 years old, I was in the kitchen with my mother one day. I asked her, "How do you know that you have been called to preach?" She asked, "Why?" Then I said to her, "Because it stays on my mind." Then she said to me, "When you say your prayers, ask the Lord what He wants you to do." So, I did just that, and the more I asked the Lord what He wanted me to do, the stronger became my desire to preach. Even though I was too young to understand it at the time, my mother introduced me to the hallways of faith. Through her prayers and faith, the miraculous power of was demonstrated in my life.

Chapter 2 – Philip's Blindness

John 14:8-10

"Philip saith unto him, Lord, shew us the Father, and it sufficeth us.
Jesus saith unto him, Have I been so long time with you, and yet hast thou not known me, Philip? he hath seen me hath seen the Father; and how sayest thou then, Shew us the Father?
Believest thou not that I am in the Father, and the Father in me? the words that I speak unto you I speak not of myself: but the father that dwelleth in me, he doeth the works."

From a young child, I knew there was "something" different about me. I could not articulate it but I knew there was "a reason" why instead of playing outside with other kids my age, I spent much of my time alone. There was a reason my family has always supported and respected me. They never criticized me or said I was too young. There was a reason why they never called me a phony. Even my schoolmates and teachers said they saw "something" different in me, and they were also respectful toward me.

I believe I always wanted to please the Lord, and I always loved to go to church. I was a praying person before I became a preacher. I thank God for prayer. Many of the temptations of my peers were never really my temptations. For some reason, I just wanted to seek a better understanding of God.

People called me "Rev," short for reverend, even when I did not know I had a calling to preach. Many times I would go in the field and preach to the cows, to the chickens and to the trees.

I was inquisitive about God, and for some reason, the concept and the mystery of God appealed to me. I believed that He was real, but I wanted to know and understand more about who He really is. One day I became introduced to that "something," that someone, that presence, that sovereignty, to the God that wanted to use my life.

As a young teenager, I began to travel with the True Light Gospel Singers. My mother was confident that Rev. Herman Traylor – the lead singer for the group- and other members of the gospel group would take care of her young son. Unknowingly through all of this, God was using these performances to draw me closer to Him and fulfill His divine purpose for my life.

Before the singing engagements, I would pray before the True Light Gospel Singers sang. I always had a yearning to pray. I think I received that anointing from my parents because my father would gather us for family prayer every Sunday morning, and again my mother was a prayer warrior.

I recall many times, donned in a white short-sleeved shirt, I was put on a chair so I could be seen by the audience as I prayed. Some adults said I petitioned the Lord as if I was talking directly to God and already knew Him. But, much like Phillip, Jesus' disciple, I witnessed the miracles He performed in my life, but I lacked the experience that would help me to know God better. Although I was knowledgeable of Him, I also realized that I needed a deeper experience with Him. I needed a spiritual birth.

In 1956, I accepted Christ as my Savior and Lord, and became baptized, at Ray Avenue Baptist Church in eastern New Orleans. Rev. Irvin Stafford, Sr. was the Founding Pastor. My natural birth is special to me, but my spiritual birth brought about the newness that made an extraordinary change in my life. With my regeneration came a new life with a godly purpose.

Finally, I began preaching the precious gospel of Jesus Christ at the age of fourteen, and I became a licensed minister in 1960. I was also the first of my siblings to be called into the preaching ministry. At that point, I needed spiritual guidance. So, the Lord assigned Pastor Henry Harris Hammond of the Little Rock Baptist Church to take me as a young preacher under his wings. Pastor Hammond loved, mentored, and groomed me until I was ready for Kingdom ministry, and he ordained me in 1964. I accepted Pastor Hammond and his wife, Mother Anna Martin Hammond, as my spiritual parents, and they were great examples of godly leaders. Some years later, they became the godparents of my son, Johnny Marlon, Jr.

Pastor Hammond was my first mentor and the "hammer" that helped to hold my anchor down.

This man of wisdom and helped me to keep my feet on the ground until the Lord called him to his eternal rest in 1982. After Pastor Hammond's departure from this earth, I was often comforted with the words of his favorite scripture in Matthew 18:3 which says, "Verily I say unto you, unless you are converted and become as little children, you will by no means enter the kingdom of heaven." This scripture always reminds me to have a humble attitude and to depend on the Lord as a little child depends on his father to provide all his needs.

Receiving the Lord in faith and submitting to His will and His teachings was my next step through the hallways of faith. Decades later, I continue to enjoy watching the mysteries of God unfold.

Bishop Johnny Marlon Williams Sr.

Chapter 3 – Elisha's Willingness
1 Kings 19:19-20

"So he departed thence, and found Elisha the son of Sha'phat, who was plowing with twelve yoke of oxen before him, and he with the twelfth; and Elijah passed by him, and cast his mantle upon him.
And he left the oxen, and ran after Elijah, and said, Let me, I pray thee, kiss my father and my mother, and then I will follow thee. And he said unto him, Go back again: for what have I done to thee?"

Bishop Johnny Marlon Williams Sr.

Detroit, MI 1968

As the Lord placed various mentors in my path, I accepted their mantles as Elisha did with Elijah, his spiritual mentor, and I made a strong commitment to use their words of wisdom to contribute to my success as a pastor, overseer, and teacher of the Word of God.

Even as a young man, I believed that being prepared when delivering the Word of God was essential. God will place people in our lives to help us along the way but we must do our part to prepare ourselves for service. One of my mottos is "You must do your homework." It is vital that those called to be carriers of the Word must stay in God's classroom and study to rightly divide the Word of Truth. My obedience to the call of Christ into the ministry opened the door to an unquenchable knowledge of our Creator.

Although, I earned my Bachelor and Master of Theology degrees at The Christian Bible College and was merited a Doctor of Divinity degree from the Inter-Baptist Theological Center of Houston, Texas, I continuously sought mentorship in ministry.

In the winter of 1968, my wife, Ruth, and I decided to move to Detroit, Michigan. Her uncle Weber and his wife lived there, and they encouraged us to come to Detroit to acquire better paying jobs at that time. So, we packed our belongings and took our baby daughter, Lyntrel, with us to the big Motor City. Detroit was definitely a different experience. The winters were long and extremely cold, and we had to adjust to the culture of the city.

The first church we wanted to visit was the New Bethel Baptist church on the west side of Detroit. The renowned Reverend C.L. Franklin was pastor. After meeting Reverend Franklin and numerous visitations to the church services, we united our membership with the New Bethel church family. For some reason, Rev. Franklin favored me and accepted me as one of his sons in the ministry.

Rev. Franklin invited me to his home to have Bible Study and he shared some of his pastoral experiences with me. He also shared some of his mistakes and gave me wise advice. He became another one of my ministerial mentors. Many people say my preaching style is similar to that of Rev. Franklin. One of the lessons I learned from Rev. Franklin's tutelage was to always be approachable. Jesus was successful and received by the multitudes during His earthly ministry because He was approachable. When His disciples tried to turn the mothers away with their children because they felt Jesus was too busy to bless the little children, Jesus said to them in Matthew 19:14-15, ...suffer the little children come to Me, and forbid them not: for of such is the kingdom of heaven. And He laid His hands on them...

Throughout my years of spiritual service, I continue to remember to demonstrate that quality throughout my life.

Bishop Johnny Marlon Williams Sr.

Throughout my pastoral journey, I have been blessed to serve as pastor of the following churches: Tree of Life Baptist Church in Detroit, Michigan (1968-1973); Old Greenwood Baptist Church in Greenwood, Louisiana (1974-1976); Greater Little Rock Baptist Church in New Orleans, Louisiana (1976-1989); founding pastor of Body of Christ Temple in New Orleans, Louisiana (1991-

2005); and founding pastor of Living Faith Baptist Cathedral in Hueytown, Alabama (2007 – Present). My family and I relocated to Alabama after experiencing the loss of our home and church building by Hurricane Katrina.

Because I submitted to mentorship, God allowed others to acknowledge me. God blessed me to receive awards such as: the Pastoral Leadership Award; Louisiana Legislature Award; Man of Purpose and Vision; the Mayor's Honorary Citizen Award; and C.M. Christar Award "Sermon of the Year" for "What If Mary Would Have Had an Abortion?"

Let me admonish you, if you ever want to go anywhere in God do not exalt yourself. Submit to God and He will exalt you.

Like Elisha, I had no problem dropping everything to follow a noteworthy leader. I have learned many useful nuggets of wisdom relating to pastoral leadership and the preaching ministry from Rev. Franklin and other great men of God.

Like Elisha, I was also ready for God to use me. He took me from a rural town in Louisiana and brought me before the presence of great renowned preachers and leaders.

To walk through the hallways of faith, you must submit to faith; submit to knowing God will take care of you. I have wondered what would have happened in my life had I not chosen to humble my ambitions to follow God and acquiesce to mentorship.

I Believe I Will Testify

"When it's too hard for us, it's Just Right for God."
-Gracie Williams Lyman

Bishop Johnny Marlon Williams Sr.

My sister Gracie's account of a testimony of a supporter:

At one time or another, many have shared testimonies of Bishop Williams's love, generosity and faith.

A relative simply had to share with me how Bishop, became her family's hero. She was six months pregnant and was placed on complete bed rest by her physician. The doctor's instructions were "she was to keep her feet elevated and her head back."

With a large smile she beamed, "Bishop would come over to our home to check on me. He would say get dressed. After taking me out to the seafood restaurant to get me delicious New Orleans Oyster Po-Boy, it was back home and back into bed. During those three months, he was often there to pray for me; asking the Lord to allow me to carry our baby to full term. He truly encouraged me. What love and devotion! God heard and answered his prayers. At the appointed time we gave birth to a healthy son."

She continued her discourse by saying her entire family adored him. Even as a young man he was special. He carried himself with such dignity. He often spoke words of prophecy to my husband and I, my mother and my children that came to pass. This man of God, Johnny Williams, is a true prophet.

During his early years, our first born son learned to love and admire Bishop. He would use a broom as a microphone to imitate Bishop Johnny preaching. As he grew older, he would follow him around New Orleans to different churches to hear him preach. I believe that today, my son is a great husband, father and son because of the influence of Bishop Williams on his life.

My sister concluded by saying, "We owe God all the praise and to Bishop much gratitude."

Bishop Johnny Marlon Williams Sr.

Chapter 4 – The Will of My Father

Matthew 12:15

"But when Jesus knew it, he withdrew himself from thence: and great multitudes followed him, and he healed them all;"

Bishop Johnny Marlon Williams Sr.

The will of God is not always popular and sometimes it is intimidating, but we must do it to advance in our walk with God. Sometimes God will test our commitment to Him by telling us to do things that may not necessarily make sense to us. Even if it does not make sense, do it anyway. What prayer and the gospel don't do cannot be done.

Years after the death of our Methodist Pastor father, I became the newly designated Spiritual leader of the family. God, Himself, chose me as Bishop of our family. What an awesome pair of shoes to refill. I was truly humbled by the appointment and believed I lacked the experienced needed for the work that was cut out for me.

My sister, Gracie, has been the magnet that can draw our family together. She is the gatherer that delivers the clarion and the glue that helps to hold us together.

God spoke to her to share with the family of this appointment. On July 7, 2007 she penned this communication to the entire Williams' family leaders of this divine nomination.

"Glory Hallelujah To God!!"
It is with the joy of the Lord that I greet you. The devastation of Hurricane Katrina has caused many of us to be separated geographically, but not within our hearts. This is why I am writing: God has placed it upon my heart to write you concerning the Bishop of our family: Johnny Marlon Williams, Sr. Like many of us he has also been through the storm.

For over forty years, he has preached the gospel of Jesus Christ to our family and countless others all over America. At one time or another he has served as our pastor; he christened our babies; performed marriages of our young and older people; has been available during crisis and tragedies to comfort and counsel; made pleas to judges and courts to have our loved ones released from prison cells; delivered the eulogy at the home going celebration of many family members; in other words, this servant has served our family quite well.

The Spirit of the Lord says that Johnny Marlon Williams, Sr., is the Bishop of our family. Now I am asking you to be a blessing to our own. Please, honor him with your very best financial blessing now and prayerfully consider making a monthly gift for the next six (6) months.

Let us unite and do this in an overflowing and timely manner to be a blessing to our man of God, Bishop Johnny and his lovely wife, Lady Ruth.

I thank you very kindly for allowing us to share with you the opportunity to be a part of this great effort. I know the Lord will bless you mightily.

Yours in Christ Jesus,
Evangelist Gracie Williams Lyman"

The response of our family to this matter was overwhelming. Had I not obeyed God, I would not have been in position to meet the needs of the family in this capacity.

Walking through the hallways of faith involves seeking God and understanding what the will of God is for you and pursuing it.

Bishop Johnny Marlon Williams Sr.

Chapter 5 – Mary's Obedience

Luke 1:38

"And Mary said, Behold the handmaid of the Lord; be it unto me according to thy word. And the angel departed from her."

In 1973, the Supreme Court ruled that most states' anti-abortion laws were unconstitutional. The pro-choice group was elated over the decision, while various Christian groups and pro-life groups opposed the decision. The controversy between the groups intensified during the 1980s; some used strong language and others proposed violence.

One morning, between the hours of two and three o'clock AM, the Holy Spirit woke me up as usual; that is the quality time He has designated for me to commune with Him. As I sat meditating on the Word of God, I heard a clear and calm voice say to me, "What if Mary would have had an abortion?" A few days later, as I watched a discussion about the abortion conflict on the evening news, that same voice spoke to me again and said, "What if Mary would have had an abortion?" That moment, I realized the Lord had given me another message to deliver to His people. He wanted me to challenge Satan with His Word of Truth on the sermon titled *What If Mary Would Have Had an Abortion?*

I can recall one testimony that was told by a single mother whose name I will not reveal. After many years, this testimony still touches my heart this very day.

One evening I received a phone call at home. The young mother began to speak tearfully and said how much she thanked the Lord for directing her to go to church on the Sunday that I recorded the sermon *What If Mary Would Have Had an Abortion?* She said she had not planned to attend the worship service because she was depressed after learning earlier that she was pregnant. She said, "I could not give birth to another child because I was neither financially or circumstantially prepared. Even though I heard the message from the Lord, I made arrangements for the abortion anyway and found myself on the table about to have my baby aborted." She told how the abortionist entered the room after she was prepped for the procedure, and how she began to look at the instruments the doctor was going to use to kill her baby. She said then she heard a voice repeating the words "What if Mary Would Have Had an Abortion?" Suddenly, she said she started screaming and jumped off the table. The doctor and his assistant asked her what was wrong. Still crying she said, "I can't do this. It's wrong. I heard that sermon and a voice just spoke to me. I heard that sermon and you should hear it too," she said. "Then I got dressed and rushed home." Listening to that message from the Lord saved her unborn child's life. Today, that same baby is a college graduate and has a lovely family.

My sister, Mary, also shared this life-saving account with me. She said a young unmarried teenager became pregnant. Her mother was concerned about her daughter's life and reputation being ruined. The mother wanted her daughter to finish school and get married before she had children. She felt the pregnancy would be an embarrassment to her family. Plus, she was concerned about how her daughter could take care of a baby. So, she decided to take her daughter to have an abortion. The daughter felt she had no choice but to yield to her mother's wish. She had to allow the innocent child growing inside her body to die. When they arrived to the abortion clinic, the mother said that as she was about to sign the papers for the abortion, she heard a voice saying, "You are about to sign away a life". Then the mother said she remembered hearing the word from the sermon *What If Mary Would Have Had an Abortion?* She said she laid the pen down and took her daughter home.

Again, the Lord used that sermon to prevent another murder and to save another innocent baby's life. Later, that sermon was awarded as "Sermon of the Year".

Many more mothers have told their stories of how their children are alive today because they heard the sermon God gave to me personally.

A few other memorable sermons that have impacted the lives of many are:

Seeing God Through a Narrow Window
When Jesus Is in Your Boat
David's Testimony in the 23rd Psalms
Don't Lose Your Soul Over Crumbs

A husband confessed that he and his wife decided not to get a divorce after he heard the sermon *Don't Lose Your Soul Over Crumbs.* He said he realized that their disputes were only crumbs and were not worth dissolving their marriage. After witnessing so many testimonies relating to the sermons the Lord gave to me, I am so grateful that I walked in obedience to the voice of God and spread His truth, even though the topics may not have been popular or favorable.

Walking through the hallways of faith involves being attentive and submissive to God's voice. Sometimes God awakens us in the middle of the night to speak to us; we should sit up and hear what He is speaking. Sometimes it is difficult to perceive the impact the words we speak have on other people's lives, but if God is using us, then the words we speak will bring deliverance to somebody's life.

Bishop Johnny Marlon Williams Sr.

Walking through the Hallways of Faith

Back Cover Dedication:

This Album dedicated to my lovely wife Ruth and our children.

Also to: Dr. Welton Washington, Pastor, New Birth Baptist Church
Dr, Freddie H Dunn, Pastor, New Hope Baptist Church

Dr. J. C. Profit, Pastor, Stronger Hope Baptist Church

Dr. W.E. Hausey, Pastor, St. John Institutional Baptist Church

Mr. O'Neil Swanson of Detroit, Michigan

Dr. Author P. Clay, Pastor, Little Zion Baptist Church of Kenner, Louisiana

Mr. & Mrs. I.D.Sanders of Greenwood, Louisiana

Dr. D. N. Mesire, Christan Temple Baptist Church

Rev. & Mrs. Eddie Williams, my parents, whom I love so much.
And
Dr. H.H. Hammond, Pastor Emeritus, Greater Little Baptist Church of New Orleans, Louisiana

Bishop Johnny Marlon Williams Sr.

Chapter 6 – A Time of Pentecost

1 Corinthians 16:7-9

"For I will not see you now by the way; but I trust to tarry a while with you, if the Lord permit.
But I will tarry at Ephesus until Pentecost.
For a great door and effectual is opened unto me, and there are many adversaries."

Acts 2:3-4

"And there appeared unto them cloven tongues like as of fire, and it sat upon each of them.
And they were all filled with the Holy Ghost, and began to speak with other tongues, as the Spirit gave utterance."

I recall the day the Lord manifested Himself to me through His precious Holy Ghost. I had been preaching since I was twelve years old, and I had already been serving as pastor for several years.

One regular Tuesday Morning Prayer Hour at the "Rock" (the "Rock" was the name members of Greater Little Rock Baptist Church affectionately called their church), some of the sisters had gathered to give God thanks and to intercede for the needs of those in the body of Christ. The prayer warriors kneeled and used several of the pews as their personal altars. The faithful few prayer warriors were on their posts.

My sister Mary, Mother Hattie Barnes, Sister Jerri Allen, Sister Beverly Preston and I were some of the believers in attendance. There were sounds of praise, petitions, and worship in the house of God. There were also humbled groans and graduating moans to outright cries of hope in the sanctuary. The presence of the Lord was there. I was kneeling at the altar when all of a sudden I began to speak in a language they had never heard me speak before. The sound became louder as I rolled to the floor.

The other sisters out of fear asked, "What is wrong with him?" One thought I was having a seizure, and another concluded I was sick. They had never witnessed any one speak in a heavenly language. But Sis Mary assured them that I was okay. I was okay! I had just received the Holy Ghost! I could not stop speaking in that heavenly language because my spirit was talking directly to God. What an experience!

I had seen our mother and some of our sisters move under the power of the Holy Ghost, but at that moment I was doing the same. Afterwards, other believers received the gift of the Holy Spirit with the evidence of speaking in an unknown tongue.

Bishop Johnny Marlon Williams Sr.

Many did not believe people in the Baptist churches could receive the gift of the Holy Ghost. I do not think the Lord cares about the name on the church building. The Baptist church is a great place for the Lord to endow His believers with the Holy Ghost. Glory!

As you walk through the hallways of faith, you must be endowed with God's Holy Spirit.

Chapter 7 – Signs and Wonders
Mark 16:20

"And they went forth, and preached everywhere, the Lord working with them, and confirming the word with signs following. Amen."

As pastor, servant and carrier of the word of God, I must believe in the in power in which I preach. I believe in the power of prayer. God has not failed me. By God's grace, I have prayed for many and God answered by performing miracles. I boast in the power of God. It is His power that heals.

There was one young lady who was a member of Little Rock Baptist Church. She and her husband had been praying for years to have a child, but nothing happened. At one worship service during altar call, I prayed to God that the young lady would be blessed and that she and her husband would be blessed with a child. Yes, the Lord heard His servant's petition, and she gave birth to a beautiful baby boy. Today, that baby boy is now a young man who has a prestigious job at a large corporation in Dallas, Texas.

Many former members, family, neighbors, and others can testify of their healing through the power of God. I recall one sister wore a black glove with her attire. No one ever mentioned why she wore the glove but later we found it was because she could not use that hand. I recall praying for her, she took the glove off and began to use her hand.

When Satan attacked my sister, Eyvonne, with breast cancer, I told my sister, Gracie, "Sister, Satan is no respecter of persons." The physicians suggested she get her affairs in order because she only had a few months to live. She went to the funeral home, made the final arrangements ….and the saints prayed."

"But during a service, the Holy Spirit allowed me to call on her. I said to her, "Sister, Satan is no respecter of persons. Do you believe in the power of prayer?" Eyvonne answered, "Yes."

Bishop Johnny Marlon Williams Sr.

The Lord permitted me to lay hands on her and pray. The Christian believers began to also pray in agreement. She went back to the doctors; the cancer was gone. No more cancer showed up in her mammogram. That was more than thirty years ago. She is still rejoicing and praising God for her healing."

Many experience God's miraculous power every day to include salvation which is one of the greatest miracles a person could ever receive. As a pastor, I love preaching in the open outdoors more than inside a building behind a pulpit but I have come to understand that the miraculous healing and saving power of God operates both inside and outside of the church walls.

One of my greatest evangelical encounters occurred in a state penitentiary. As pastor of The Body of Christ Temple, our outreach team had a complete mobile church. I had a burden for souls. I was a champion for the least accepted, the less privileged, the poor and the lost. Whether at Public Housing Complexes or Prison yards, any place I could park that large black Church on Wheels we were ready.

One of the trucks transported a beautiful Hammond Organ, a complete set of drums, the speaker's stand, huge audio speakers and other pieces of equipment. I was prepared for the souls that accepted Christ. A trailer had been specially designed to hold the baptismal pool, complete with water that the church truck towed behind it. The Angola State Penitentiary was only one of many places where The Church on Wheels ministry was set up for witnessing, worshipping, preaching, teaching, and baptizing. During one visit to the state prison, the prison choir sang to the glory of God. My message of love and forgiveness pierced the hearts of the spiritually hungry crowd. Tearful souls came in submission to the Lord. The altar was fruitful. Nineteen were baptized.

The trip up from New Orleans and down a snake-winding road that led to the state prison, had been more than worth the effort. Almost to the end of the service, a young man came up to receive the Lord. He expressed his desire to be saved and accepted the Lord as his Savior and wanted to be baptized. He said to me, "You don't know who I am, do you?" I answered him, "No, I don't." The young man went onto tell me, "I'm Shawn Williams, I married your niece Kim. I'm in this place for killing her while I was under the influence of drugs."

For a moment the wind was taken out of my sail. This

young man had been serving a life sentence without the possibility of parole for the last six years. Kim's four-year-old son had told the police that his father put the gun to his mother's head and said POW (shooting Kim). He had been found guilty of the murder of my beautiful niece, Kim Ann. I didn't know what to do. I had never been faced with anything like this in my life. God did a quick work in my heart. I had to forgive Shawn of his wrong, just as our savior forgave me. On that day, he was looking for forgiveness from me and I could not let God down. Yes, I forgave him and he went away at peace. I began to glorify the Lord for giving me such an opportunity to snatch another soul from the clutches of Satan and out of hell. Not even the bars of the prison could hold this young man back any longer. Hallelujah!! That was a powerful experience.

Through evangelistic efforts, the good news of Christ's love for humanity reached many lost souls as God's word penetrated their hearts. God afforded numerous opportunities for His Gospel to be shared, and for the Truth to be heard.

To walk through the hallways of faith involves believing in the power in which we preach and the sovereignty of which we testify. It sometimes involves confessing your own faults and receiving forgiveness so that others will be saved.

Bishop Johnny Marlon Williams Sr.

I Believe I Will Testify

I came to faith in God and the Lord Jesus Christ under the preaching and teaching of Bishop Johnny M. Williams, Sr. My first encounter with the Bishop was one Sunday in the fall of 1978 at the Greater Little Rock Baptist Church in New Orleans, Louisiana. I had visited the church that Sunday to hear my cousin, the Reverend Michael Polk, an associate minister under Pastor Williams, preach the message that day. At the time, I was not a believer in God, nor of the Lord Jesus Christ; but my cousin kept pestering me about coming to hear him preach, and so I did.

As is common in most churches, at the end of the sermon (which I'm sure was very nice), Pastor Williams extended an invitation to Christian discipleship. Here was the opportunity for anyone having been moved by the message, and desiring to accept Jesus as their Savior, and to become a member of the Church, to come forward and so acknowledge it. I never moved!! I had no intention of joining that church, or any other church. I did not believe in God!!

Bishop Johnny Williams, however, being the Spirit-led man of faith that I later discovered him to be, apparently had set his spiritual eyes on me. He labored mightily in extending that invitation. He must have given every reason and every Scripture under the sun about how one can be saved, and why one should want to be saved. But I wasn't hearing any of it. The sermon was over and as far as I was concerned, it was time to go.

But, the Bishop was not through just yet. He looked at me, and then pointed to me, and said, "young man, you right there! Are you willing to come up, and just let me pray for you? I just want to pray for you." How do you say no to that with the whole church looking at you!!?? Of course I went up; and I let him pray for me. I don't know what he prayed _ I wasn't listening! I don't know how long he prayed; I didn't really care. I just wanted it to be over. Then, when he finally finished praying, he asked this question, "Now, are you willing to make a decision for Jesus, and to become a member of the Church?" I already had my answer ready. Almost before he could finish asking the question my mouth was fixed to say No! But what came out was "Yyyess".

The Church went ballistic. People were on their feet thanking and praising God. My cousin and others were shaking my hand and grinning. And I was standing there wondering, "What in the world just happened? What did I just do?" It wasn't until later that day when my cousin helped me to understand that when this man of God prayed for me and my salvation, the Spirit of God heard him, and moved in this special way to bring me into the fold. That was thirty-eight years ago, and I have been worshipping, and praising, and serving God ever since.

My story, however, is not unique. Over the years that I've served under Bishop Williams, and with him, I have seen this scenario played out time and time again.

Scores of people have come to faith in Jesus Christ under his preaching and teaching and his prayer ministry. He fervently believes that what the gospel and prayer can't do just can't be done. If he can't preach the hell out of you, he'll pray the hell out of you; or he'll pray you out of whatever bad situation you happen to find yourself in.
But, in order to be effective, prayer must always be coupled with faith, unwavering trust that God will do just what He said He'll do.

Prayer without faith is a waste of time. And faith is something that Johnny Williams has plenty of. But wait, not just faith. Crazy faith!! He actually believes that whatever he asks God for, because he asks in faith, God will absolutely do it for him. When he prays for your deliverance, he expects you to be delivered. When he prays for your healing, he expects you to be healed. When he prays for your prosperity, he expects you to prosper, and to become a blessing to others. When he asked God for a church building from which to witness and minister "debt free" in a city in which he'd never lived, and from a people he did not previously know, he simply trusted God for it; and guess what God gave it to him.

Bishop Williams has always said to those to whom he ministered that you sometimes have to put prayers in the bank. You never know what's going to come up in your life. A time may come when you don't know to pray, or you simply can't pray. But when you have prayers in God's bank, like a good savings account, you'll have something to draw from to get your breakthrough. That's his kind of faith in what God will do.

His faith paid off mightily in late February, 2014 when he suffered cardiac arrest in his sleep. He was in no position to pray about his situation; but he had prayers in the bank; and a record of unswerving faith that God will always come through for you, not matter what the circumstances might be. God came through for him that day; and every day since. I'm glad that He did; because Bishop Johnny Marlon Williams, Sr., my own father in the ministry, lived to tell us his own story of *Walking Through the Hallways of Faith.*

Rev. James R. Willis, Jr. Pastor
Carver Desire Baptist Church
New Orleans, Louisiana

Bishop Johnny Marlon Williams Sr.

Chapter 8 – The Waters of Faith

Matthew 14:28

"And Peter answered him and said, Lord, if it be thou, bid me to come unto thee on the water."

Mark 9:23

"And Jesus said unto him. If thou canst believe, all things are possible to him that believeth."

Just two months after I told my sister Gracie that I wanted our niece Nicole Jones to write my life story, I shared the news with my family that I had prostate cancer. I'm told, my sister Gracie went to sleep praying, and awakened the next morning supplicating on my behalf.

Each of my sisters called to check on me out of concern. My voice was the same, positive and strong. I told them, I have nothing to complain about, "I am blessed because I am on top of dirt and dirt is not on top of me."

I shared with my sisters that there appeared to be two spots on my prostate but they detected the spots early and that in six weeks they would do surgery and remove the prostate. My wife and I agreed to the surgery.

I told my family that there is nothing to worry about. It probably will be a one-day surgery.

I reassured my family that I was alright.

I had commissioned Gracie to write my biography and gave her the instructions to 'hurry.' I wanted to have the book completed by August of this summer. In another phone conversation, I gave Gracie the details of my home going celebration. I told her that I wanted her to lead the family in and preside, and I wanted my daughter Lynn, to preach my Eulogy. I had ordained Lyntrel Davis a few months prior to my preparations. In the same rite, I placed her as assistant pastor of Living Faith Baptist Cathedral.

With all this unique preparation, my family believed my prognosis was known to me prior to telling them and that I was trying to protect the family from worrying about my condition.

If He did it before he can do it again. He did do it... and He can do it again!

In the meantime, the prayer warriors flooded the altars. Our altars were in several states. Two of my sisters were praying in Birmingham; others were in Louisiana, Texas, Mississippi, Arkansas, and other places. Many of us came together on the conference prayer lines five days a week. Yes, they knew how to petition heaven.

Several weeks later, I underwent surgery at eight thirty a.m. My sisters had already been praying since they learned of my sickness and the date of the procedure, but they started praying again.

Three hours later... another praise report. God did it again! We thank You, Lord Jesus! Everything went well. The doctors said all of the cancer cells were removed and I would not need to take chemotherapy treatments nor radiation. My doctor said he wanted to keep me overnight for observation. The next day I was discharged.

God will always help us. God will heal us. However, we must understand that the hallways of faith are transitory. Our journeys all come to an end. As daunting the task, whether in sickness or health, we must learn to set our business in order and prepare successors to

Bishop Johnny Marlon Williams Sr.

take our place. We know that when the Lord bids us to come He will be with us through every step of our lives.

Chapter 9– The Chapter of Ruth

Ruth 1:16

"And Ruth said. Intreat me not to leave thee, or to return from following after thee: for whiter thou goest, I will go; and where thou lodgest, I will lodge: thy people shall be my people, and thy God my God:"

Abigail – A woman of good understanding
I Samuel 25: 28

"I pray thee, forgive the trespass of thine handmaid: for the Lord will certainly make my lord a sure house; because my lord fighteth the battles of the Lord, and evil hath not been found in thee all thy days."

Special Introduction:

I could not write a book without including the significant feature that helps to make my life complete...my wife, Ruth. Most of my fondest memories include her in them.

Ruth and I met when we were very young and she has supported me throughout all of the years I have known her. She has always been smart; and I have always admired her ambition. Ruth is soft spoken and quiet but she is a powerful force and has no problem letting me know when I am wrong

I wanted her to write her story but I beseech you as you walk through the hallways of faith to always appreciate those who have supported you along the way.

Dr. Ruth Washington Williams

A Wife Named Ruth

I am Ruth, the wife of Bishop Johnny M. Williams, Sr. I am so grateful to the Almighty God for allowing me this opportunity to share a portion of our story.

We were married in August 1967 in New Orleans, Louisiana, and we were honored to have my late father, Rev. Welton Washington and the late Rev. Henry H. Hammond, to perform our marriage ceremony on that very special day.

I was in my junior year at Dillard University in New Orleans when we were married. Of course, we started a family and my focus was on being a mother instead of focusing on the books. The Lord blessed us with four of our biological children: Lyntrel, Angela, Lashawn , Johnny Jr., and our oldest son, Troy, who has a very special place in our lives.

As our children grew older, my husband encouraged me to go back to college to complete my bachelors degree in Education and later my masters and Doctorate degrees in Counseling.

As a preacher's kid, I was fully aware of the challenges that so many pastor's families must face on a daily bases. Those experiences from my childhood prepared me for our ministry as spiritual leaders in the church.

I am so thankful for my husband who is always serious about his walk with the Lord and is known for saying what he means and means what he says. Of course, there were a few phases in our lives when he made some not so good decisions which caused some stressful moments, but his good outweighed his not so good. Our love for each other and most importantly having Christ as head of our marriage triangle and our lives, made it possible to proceed victoriously through our temporary valleys in life.

In spite of Satan's attempts to prevent my husband from fulfilling God's assignment for his life, God always received the glory, and my husband always came through successfully by defeating Satan in his tracks.

The Testimony:

On Wednesday morning, February 26, 2014, at 1:00 a.m., I awoke to strange sounds coming from my husband. At first I thought he was kidding around with me as he does sometimes. But then I realized that this was serious. When I turned on the light, I saw an unusual look on his face, and he was making that same strange sound. I called him several times, but he did not respond to me. Immediately, I called 9-1-1. The 9-1-1 operator began to instruct me how to administer CPR until the emergency unit arrived. Suddenly, he stopped breathing. It was almost as if the earth had stopped turning on its axis. I could not believe this was happening. I kept calling his name, but he did not respond. Then the paramedics arrived and started working on him, and the police officer asked me to walk in the next room while they worked on my Bishop.

The paramedics used an External Heart Defibrillator to shock his heart back to beating on its own. Then they rushed him to the nearest hospital that was just a few miles from our home. But, by the time I arrived to the emergency room, the doctor said they should send him to University of Alabama in Birmingham (UAB) Hospital because they could better treat him for the cardiac arrest he was experiencing. So, immediately, they transported my husband.

When I arrived there, they had already taken him to the Cardiac Intensive Care Unit (CICU). The doctor explained to me that they performed a Brain CAT SCAN and my husband's brain scan showed 28 percent brain damage- as a result of the lack of oxygen to his brain when his heart stopped beating. They needed to reduce his body temperature to prevent further brain damage and requested my permission. I agreed to the recommendation, and his body temperature was lowered to 89.66 degrees for several days.

My husband was on life support machines for four weeks and remained in CICU for four weeks. I was informed that if he survived, he would be in a vegetative state.

The heart specialist explained to me that out of one hundred people who have Cardiac arrests, only five live. Out of the five who live, only two can live a quality life. The doctor finally explained it would take about two to three years to recover totally from his medical condition. But God said not so! God, who has the final answer, did not agree with the norm.

There were people from so many states around our country who were praying for his recovery and Bishop was eventually released from the CICU.

After being discharged from the CICU, Bishop was in rehab for an additional four weeks, and continued with rehab a year after leaving the hospital. Although Bishop was in the hospital and rehab, his ministry never stopped. God was still using him behind the scenes.

On the day Bishop was being discharged from rehab, one of the nurses stopped us and expressed how Bishop's weeks in rehab blessed her. She said each morning Bishop would wake up, he would be in his room praying and preaching as if he were preaching to a congregation. She said, overtime she found herself intentionally venturing in his area to overhear him speak. She testified, that the messages he preached brought deliverance to her and helped her to overcome some obstacles she had been experiencing at home.

God was meeting the needs of someone else who crossed our path, while He was also rewarding our faith.

God has really blessed Bishop throughout that entire episode to fully recover. He still serves as pastor, delivers the Word during the Sunday Worship Services, and he is still praying for those who believe in the power of prayer.

Oh yes, the last brain scan Bishop had to take revealed no brain damage and his brain appeared normal. God answered the fervent prayer of the righteous. I am blessed to have witnessed the performance of God's miraculous power in our lives. Praise the Almighty God.

Bishop Johnny Marlon Williams Sr.

Chapter 10–Revelations
Matthew 16:17

"And Jesus answered and said unto him, Blessed art thou, Simon Bar-jo'na: for flesh and blood hath not revealed it unto thee, but my Father which is in heaven."

Hallways are not permanent destinations. They are avenues to various destinations. As you walk through the hallways, do not get stuck. Stay focused. Learn as many lessons along the way. Allow God to reveal His wisdom to you as He unfolds His purpose in your life.

Again, I admonish you as you walk through the hallways of faith, follow good demonstrators of faith; receive the Lord in faith and submit to His will; seek God and understand His will for your life. Be attentive and submissive to the voice of the Lord. Believe in the power of which you breach; do not be afraid to forgive. Become endowed with the Holy Spirit. Be attentive and submissive to mentorship. Always appreciate those who have supported you along the way.

With you I share this wisdom:

Have a love for God. Learn to talk with Him. Have a rapport with the Lord. Don't go to Him as a stranger.

Be dedicated and committed to God.

Be yourself and do not try to be anyone else. Don't rush to get anything or anywhere overnight. A shortcut will not work.

Have a prayer life. A prayer life makes you stronger and stronger.

Put God First. Acknowledge Him. Leave out "Me" and "My." It's about Him.

As my sister, Gracie, eloquently wrote, "Trust God to lead you as He brings you through the hallways of faith, to each opened door in your life."

Bishop Johnny Marlon Williams Sr.

Words to Walk by

"So then Faith Commeth by hearing and hearing by the Word of God" Roman 10:17

Hebrews 11:1-2
The substance or matter of our hope is Faith.

St John 16:23
Pray, asking God in the name of Jesus.

St John 19:30
When Christ had completed His purpose for coming to earth, He said 'It's Finished.'

II Corinthians 5:7
The life we live in Christ is one of faith.

Ephesians 3:20
God can do more than we can imagine.

Matthew 9:26
Nothing is impossible for God do.

Proverbs 3:5-6
Trust and acknowledge God for direction.

James 5:16
We must pray for each other.

II Corinthians 1:11
Our prayers help others.

Matt 1:18-25
Don't abort the promise God has birthed in you.

Luke1: 26-28
Christ's holy birth was for our redemption.

Matthew 6:12
Forgiveness is an essential part of God's plan.

Psalm 51
Cleansing through repentance brings God's mercy.

Bishop Johnny Marlon Williams Sr.

Notes:

Bishop Johnny Marlon Williams Sr.

Bishop Johnny Marlon Williams Sr.

Bishop Johnny Marlon Williams Sr.

Bishop Johnny Marlon Williams Sr.

Bishop Johnny Marlon Williams Sr.

Bishop Johnny Marlon Williams Sr.

Bishop Johnny Marlon Williams Sr.

www.ingramcontent.com/pod-product-compliance
Lightning Source LLC
Chambersburg PA
CBHW020915090426
42736CB00008B/651